My Little Golden Book About
FRIDA KAHLO

By Silvia López

Illustrated by Elisa Chavarri

The editors would like to thank Eva Recinos, arts and culture writer,
for her assistance in the preparation of this book.

A GOLDEN BOOK • NEW YORK

Text copyright © 2021 by Silvia López
Cover art and interior illustrations copyright © 2021 by Elisa Chavarri
All rights reserved. Published in the United States by Golden Books, an imprint of Random House
Children's Books, a division of Penguin Random House LLC, 1745 Broadway, New York, NY 10019.
Golden Books, A Golden Book, A Little Golden Book, the G colophon, and the distinctive gold spine
are registered trademarks of Penguin Random House LLC.
rhcbooks.com
Educators and librarians, for a variety of teaching tools, visit us at RHTeachersLibrarians.com
Library of Congress Control Number: 2019948141
ISBN 978-0-593-17542-2 (trade) — ISBN 978-0-593-17543-9 (ebook)
Printed in the United States of America
10 9 8 7 6 5 4

FRIDA KAHLO was born on July 6, 1907, just outside Mexico City, in a blue house with green shutters. Her father, Guillermo, had built the blue house—called La Casa Azul—for his wife, Matilde, and their four daughters: Matilde, Adriana, Frida, and little Cristina.

La Casa Azul's courtyard garden was perfect for exploring. Frida collected rocks, leaves, and insects. She wanted to be a doctor, although at the time, girls were not always encouraged to study.

One morning, Frida complained of a terrible pain in one leg. She had contracted polio, a disease that keeps muscles from growing properly. We now have a vaccine to prevent polio. But back then, nothing could be done.

Frida's leg became weak. She had to stay in bed for months. How boring! To entertain herself, she fogged up a window with her breath and drew a door with her finger. Then she pretended to fly out and go dancing with a secret friend.

Polio left Frida with a limp, but she was strong and independent. Her father encouraged her to play sports—even wrestling! Guillermo was a photographer. He showed her lovely buildings and taught her about Mexico's beautiful art and history. He knew his daughter was smart.

Frida was accepted to an excellent high school. There were more than two thousand boys and only thirty-five girls! She was a good student, but she was also mischievous. Frida once sneaked a donkey into school and let it wander through the halls!

One day, an artist named Diego Rivera came to the school to paint a mural.

Frida began playing pranks. She stole Diego's lunch. She made noises behind his back. But she also loved watching him work, her eyes sparkling beneath eyebrows shaped like a raven's wings.

When she was eighteen, Frida was badly hurt in an accident. After many surgeries, much of her body was placed in a cast. She had to lie on her back for months.

I paint myself because
I am so often alone...

Frida could not return to school. She set aside her dream of becoming a doctor. She could move only her arms and hands, so she decided to paint. A mirror was placed under her bed's canopy, and Frida became her own model.

When she felt better, she wanted to know whether her paintings were good. She found Diego Rivera high on a scaffold, making another mural, and asked him to look at her work.

Diego thought Frida had talent. He began visiting La Casa Azul to discuss art. Though he and Frida were very different—Frida's parents called them "the elephant and the dove"— they soon fell in love and were married.

Diego was older than Frida, and already famous. Frida accompanied him to parties wearing traditional Mexican dresses, jewelry, and hairstyles. And despite pain from her old injuries, she kept painting. Both Frida and her art were as colorful as the Mexican culture she loved.

Frida and Diego traveled to several cities in the United States so Diego could paint murals. Frida was so homesick! Her feelings came out in her art. One painting showed a dress floating in the air. This was her way of saying that although she lived in America, her heart was back home in Mexico.

An exhibition of Frida's work in New York received a lot of attention. Later, the Louvre Museum in Paris bought one of her paintings—the first piece of art by a twentieth-century Mexican artist in its collection! Frida had become world famous.

Frida and Diego moved to La Casa Azul. She filled the house with things she loved: ancient pottery, dolls, and lots of pets. There were rabbits, parrots, Mexican hairless dogs, a deer, an eagle, and a spider monkey named Fulang-Chang.

La Casa Azul was a lively place. Frida taught art to talented students. And she threw a party on every Mexican holiday!

One day, Mexico City organized a show of Frida's paintings. Her doctors said she was too sick to attend. But Frida dressed in her best outfit, hired an ambulance, and had her bed brought from La Casa Azul to the show. She greeted her admirers lying down!

Frida's health had never been good, but that didn't keep her from working every day. She made more self-portraits. She also created beautiful paintings of her family and people she admired. Frida's last painting was of watermelons, red and green, like the Mexican flag. On one slice were the words "Viva La Vida"—Long Live Life.

Frida Kahlo died in La Casa Azul on July 13, 1954. The home later became the Frida Kahlo Museum.

Today, thousands of people visit La Casa Azul each year. Her house is still full of life.

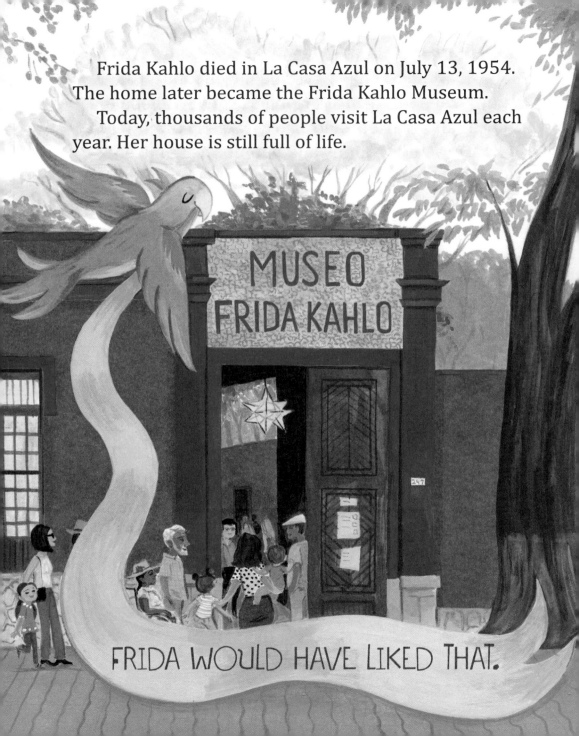

MUSEO FRIDA KAHLO

FRIDA WOULD HAVE LIKED THAT.

Have you heard a bird call out
from the branches of a rookery?
Are not the songsters of the sky
like the spirit of the child?

Mallard is my name.

I am a wetland bird.

My duck-head glitters emerald-green;

chestnut plumes enfold me like a stately cloak,

my feathery fortress against earth and sky;

round my neck I wear a proud white ring.

If you saw me pairing out across

the prairies flowing you would see

the way I spring on wing

and hie over woods and ponds.